M000085345

THE NEW RULES OF

GOLF

REDEFINING THE GAME FOR A NEW GENERATION OF PLAYERS

Dominic Bliss

DOG 'n' BONE

This book is dedicated to my brother Jez who was the first
to show me how easy it is to upset golf club members with something
as simple and innocent as the hem of a trouser, the tilt of a cap,
the swig of a hip flask, or the general cut of one's jib.

Published in 2015 by Dog 'n' Bone Books
An imprint of Ryland Peters & Small Ltd

20–21 Jockey's Fields   341 E 116th St
London WC1R 4BW   New York, NY 10029

www.rylandpeters.com

10 9 8 7 6 5 4 3 2 1

A CIP catalog record for this book is available from the Library of Congress and
the British Library.

ISBN: 978 1 909313 58 3

Printed in China

Editor: Jennifer Jahn
Golf consultant: Ben Cove
Design concept: Geoff Borin and Paul Tilby
Spread design: Paul Tilby
Illustrator: Steve Millington aka Lord Dunsby

CONTENTS

INTRODUCTION

"Know the rules well, so you can break them effectively."

So said the Dalai Lama. Chances are he wasn't talking about golf at the time, but his maxim could just as well apply to our beautiful sport. After all, it's riddled with complicated rules, conventions, and etiquette.

This book is for anyone who, at times, feels like tearing up golf's rulebook and leaving it in shreds in the rough. For any player who has ever wished to revolutionize golf's old-fashioned conventions. For golfers who would love nothing better than to bury their sport's traditional etiquette in the bunker on the 17th. These are the New Rules of Golf.

Golf should be enjoyable. There's something wrong if you spend more time worrying about the etiquette than you do lining up your shots. It's sport, not martyrdom. (Although, when you've got the yips, it can feel like martyrdom.) Yes, there will always be the old-school country clubs with their antiquated members and their elitist ways. But for the rest of us golf should be modern, forward-thinking, and—to misquote Mark Twain—a wonderful way to spoil a damn good walk.

In the following pages you'll find golf's alternative guide to etiquette: conventions designed to make the game easier, more straightforward, more stylish, less stuffy, less cheesy, and, above all, more fun to play. And most importantly—the difference with the New Rules of Golf is that there won't be a greenkeeper or a country-club manager breathing down your neck, checking you adhere to them.

Chapter One
The New Rules of Golf Match Play

1 PUTT WITH GLOVE IN BACK RIGHT POCKET

Everyone removes one's glove when it comes to putting time. It's supposed to give you a better feel of the putter. Perhaps it also allows the perspiration in the glove to dry out. However, *there's only one place to stash said glove while you're caressing golf balls into the cup and that's in your rear pant-pocket.* Not in your front pocket. And certainly not in your golf bag. The correct position is always in your rear pocket with all five fingers dangling out and neatly spaced.

There's also the bonus that, with your glove removed for a few minutes, it gives the tan on your right hand time to catch up with the tan on your left hand.

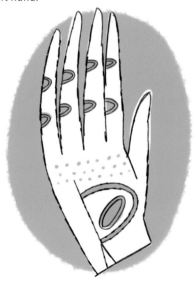

COUNT TO 30 WHEN LINING UP A PUTT

Thirty seconds is ample time to line up your putt—even on the most gruesome of greens. What is there to take into account, after all? Reading the green involves analyzing the contours, whether you're with the grain of the grass or against it, whether it's dry, wet, or spongy. You can do all this in well under half a minute. And it keeps the round swimming along nicely.

What are you waiting for? For the sun to go behind a cloud? For the stars to align? It's not like there's seismic activity on your green, so get on with it. Not that all professional players respect this rule. Sergio García, Jim Furyk, and Ben Crane are notorious for boring the underwear off fans and fellow players with their putting preparations. Ben Crane is possibly the worst culprit of all (he even gets heckled for it). Laboriously, he scrutinizes the green as if he's actually attempting to see the individual blades of grass grow. He squats down, stands up, squats down again, wiggles here, wiggles there, ponders the contours, fondles the grass, takes water samples. It wouldn't surprise anyone if he pulled out some litmus paper and subjected the green to an acidity test. You could read a book in the time it takes Crane to read a green. A very long book. With lots of very long words in it.

At the 2005 Booz Allen Classic, his progress was so frustratingly glacial that, by the time he reached the 17th green, his partner Rory Sabbatini was ready to slash his wrists. Tears of boredom stinging his eyes, he putted out of turn and stormed off to the 18th before Crane could finish the hole. It may have been unsportsmanlike, and he may have gotten booed by the crowd, but who could honestly say they wouldn't, in the same position, have done the very same thing?

The problem is that the golfing authorities won't levy fines for slow play. Yes, players get put on the clock, but they rarely have to cough up hard cash. In fact, at the time of writing, the last PGA player to be fined for slow play was Dillard Pruitt, all the way back in 1992. Ironically, Pruitt is now a rules official for the PGA Tour.

9

If the ball's in the water, then it's a goner. If it wants to have a little swim, then give it a swimsuit and some goggles and wave it goodbye. Take a drop and your one-shot penalty. *Accept it like an adult*. Even if the ball has made it %oths of the way across the lake and it's sitting up nicely in the mud, *do NOT be tempted to play it.* Think of your pride before you remove shoes and socks and roll up your pants.

Remember what happened to Jean van de Velde?

It was at the 1999 Open Championship in Carnoustie. As the tournament reached its closing stages, he was the clear leader. On the final hole, all he needed was a double bogey six to earn his place in history as the first Frenchman since 1907 to win the Open. And he was in cracking form.

Given his three-shot lead, rather unwisely, van de Velde elected to play his tee shot with his driver. The ball landed on a peninsula of land surrounded by water. To win the Open, all he had to do was play cautious golf. But instead of laying up and waiting to hit the green with his third shot, he went for it with his second. It was a crazy decision that would haunt him for the rest of his life.

The ball drifted right, struck the top of a grandstand near the green, bounced off the stone wall on the edge of the stream that snaked across the hole (Barry Burn), and then went backwards into knee-high rough. Not to worry, though. He could still win the Open. Except that he had to get over Barry Burn. On his third shot, his swing got tangled in the undergrowth and plopped the ball straight into the water. Peering into the stream, van de Velde could see his ball wasn't completely submerged.

Television commentator Peter Alliss realized what was going through the French player's mind: "He's surely not going to go and climb down in there and try to whack out of there?" Alliss asked rhetorically. "No, that would be totally ridiculous. What are you doing? What on earth are you doing? No Jean, please! Would someone kindly go and stop him. Give him a large brandy and mop him down."

Van de Velde's humiliation plummeted to new depths as he proceeded to take off his shoes and socks, roll up his pants, and wade into the stream for a closer look.

"This is beyond a joke," the incredulous Alliss continued. "He's gone gaga. To attempt to hit the ball out of there is pure madness."

Eventually, after much mulling, the by now wet-legged Frenchman plucked his ball out of the water and took a drop in the rough for his fourth stroke. He had two strokes left to win the Open.

Tragically, his next shot ended up in the bunker. The spectators didn't know whether to laugh or cry. Van de Velde looked like he wanted the ground to open up and swallow him. His bunker shot came to rest about six feet from the cup. Finally, after 23 minutes, he made the putt successfully and completed the hole. But instead of victory, he now had to come back out onto the course for a play-off with two other players—Paul Lawrie and Justin Leonard.

After such a disastrous 18th hole, van de Velde obviously didn't

stand a chance. Paul Lawrie duly took the trophy. Which all goes to prove that, should your ball end up in the water—as it surely will on more than one occasion— you must never be tempted to play it.

4 THE MULLIGAN

We all hit a god-awful tee shot now and then (we're only human, after all). *And we're all allowed a get-out-of-jail card without incurring a penalty. It's called a Mulligan.* However, just be sure it's only the one Mulligan per 18 holes that you cash in. More than that is plain greedy.

No one can agree on the true origin of the word "Mulligan." But the most widely accepted anecdote focuses on one David Mulligan, a player at the Country Club of Montreal, Canada, back in the 1920s. There are several versions of his story. One suggests that he granted himself a second tee shot on a whim, and the nickname stuck for evermore. Another tells how he was permitted a Mulligan after driving his golf partners to the club over a particularly bumpy road and a perilous bridge over the Saint Lawrence River. A third story recounts how he turned up to play and, having overslept, was granted a Mulligan since he was barely awake for his first tee shot.

Some golfers permit a Mulligan only on the first tee shot of the day—which is *great news if you haven't had time to warm up*. In certain cases, players are even allowed multiple Mulligans on the first tee, essentially hitting as many balls as they want until they are happy with their shot. A second Mulligan might be called a Finnegan, a third a Branagan, a fourth a Flanagan, and so on, until you run out of Irish last names.

Mulligans for the pros?

It's high time the professional tours embraced Mulligans, too. Unlike us mortals, for the pros it's rarely that obvious when to have a second stab at a tee shot. They are simply too good. So choosing Mulligans would necessitate a certain skill within the professional game.

Mind you, even a Mulligan wouldn't have saved Kevin Na at the 2011 Valero Texas Open. After lining up for the par-4 ninth hole, his tee shot sailed gracefully into the woods. So he took a penalty stroke and started again. His second tee shot followed a similar trajectory to his first, deep into the woods. This time he attempted to play the ball, but his shot ricocheted off a tree and struck his leg, costing him a further penalty stroke. The sublime then turned to the ridiculous as Na struggled to hack his way out of the trees. It was 12 shots before he was back on the fairway, 16 before he completed the hole and recorded the worst ever PGA score on a par 4.

Another meltdown that no Mulligan would have salvaged was John Daly's at the 1998 Bay Hill Invitational in Florida. Teeing off from the par-5 sixth hole, he spanked his first drive into the rather inconveniently located lake. So he dropped a ball and boldly attempted a very lengthy shot over the offending lake, which, of course, also ended up in a watery grave. He then dropped again and drowned a third ball and a fourth and a fifth. In all, he donated six balls to the Florida fish before he finally got the better of that body of water. Even then he had to extricate himself from a bunker before finally completing the hole and clocking up 18 shots.

Despite such a catastrophic play, Daly was surprisingly upbeat afterwards, convinced he'd set a new PGA record for the highest score on a hole. "Hey, I'm out here to break records," he said.

If you can't get the shot right with three practice swings, then what hope do you have? Any more than three and you're simply doing the greenkeepers job by trimming the grass on the tee. *Golf is supposed to be fun. Keep it moving.*

Kevin Na has earned himself the reputation of being possibly the slowest player on the PGA Tour. He fidgets, he checks his yardage book, he debates at length with his long-suffering caddie; he steps up to the ball, off the ball, then up to it again. Spectators have been known to die of old age in the time it takes him to line up his shots.

If anything, the problem of slow play in professional golf is getting worse. And that's mainly because of the authorities' reluctance to implement their rules properly. Take young golfer Andrew Loupe, for example. He often takes six, seven, ten, eleven, twelve practice swings before he pulls the trigger. Yawn.

The best way to eliminate such slothful play is to reprimand the slow-pokes. *There's nothing wrong with deploring or ridiculing your partner should he drag out his shot preparation.* Nothing wrong with moaning at the professionals, either. If spectators started heckling the likes of Na and Loupe more often, they'd soon put their foot on the gas.

Currently, if one player in a group is slow, then all his partners— even the fast players—get put on the clock. That's hardly fair, especially if you happen to find yourself playing alongside Na or Loupe.

6 DO NOT COMMAND BALLS WHILE THEY'RE IN THE AIR

Golf balls do not have ears. Shouting "Sit down! Sit down!" while your shot flies sky-high over the green is utterly pointless. It's about as useful as giving your ball a little kiss before you tee off.

Above all, do not curse at balls that sail off in the wrong direction.

As the nineteenth-century champion golfer Horace Hutchinson once famously said: "If profanity had an influence on the flight of the ball, the game of golf would be played far better than it is."

The New Rules of Golf, however, do allow you to influence the flight of your ball in the following manner: once you have struck it, *you may wiggle your arms, neck, and torso in order to guide it in the right direction. This is scientifically proven to work.*

16

As a spectator, addressing the ball while it's in the air is equally forbidden. *Do not become one of those idiots who yells, "In the hole!" at the top of his voice* every time Tiger Woods bashes it down the fairway. Shouting "Mash potato!" is even worse.

IF YOU HIT THE BALL INTO A NEIGHBORING HOLE

7

It's a common occurrence for us amateurs. You know the scenario. You're lining up for a huge tee shot, and you shank it off to the side so badly that it ends up on the fairway of a neighboring hole. What to do?

The New Rules of Golf are very clear on this. No one wants to be associated with someone who plays so badly that they hit their ball onto the wrong fairway. *It's crucial you save face for the whole of your group.* Provided no one has spotted your errant shot, you are honor-bound to walk serenely onto the next-door fairway and *play out that neighboring hole as if you had intended to play it all along.* If anyone sees you, they will assume you are in the middle of a solo round.

Once you've completed the neighboring hole, sneak back to your group and carry on with your round. And, while you're at it, complain to your buddies that it's all the course designer's fault. Curse him for cramming too many holes into too small a parcel of land.

Chapter Two
The New Rules of Golf Etiquette

Yes, we're all busy, but that doesn't change the fact that *being late for your round is unacceptably bad form.* No exceptions. Take a leaf out of Rory McIlroy's book. At the 2012 Ryder Cup, staged at Medinah Country Club in Illinois, he was almost late for his singles contest against Keegan Bradley. Confused by the US's different time zones, the Northern Irishman needed a police escort to get to the club in time. Even then he had just ten minutes to warm up before his round.

"I read the tee times on my phone. They are on Eastern Time and it's Central Time here," he offered as an excuse. "I thought I was off at 12.25pm instead of 11.25am and was making my way out of the hotel. I got a call saying, 'You have 25 minutes 'til tee off.' I was a bit worried then."

Fortunately, Medinah's finest were on hand to whisk the player straight to the venue. "In the front of the police car," McIlroy added. "At least I wasn't in the back."

Obviously very flustered, he sent his first shot for Europe into the rough. This can't have been helped by the USA fans chanting: "Central Time Zone!" Nevertheless, he quickly recovered and took the win. Had he arrived just five minutes late for the opening hole, he would have faced disqualification. The cop who helped him, Deputy Chief Pat Rollins, got serious grief from his colleagues for helping a player on the visiting team.

"I was just doing my duty," Rollins said later. "But I am getting a lot of ribbing for not driving to the wrong course or getting a flat tire."

ALCOHOL IS PERMITTED AFTER THE FIRST HOLE

Even the most liberal of golf-club managers will raise an eyebrow should you crack the booze before you've teed off the first hole. Not that there's anything wrong with drinking and driving. Part of golf's brilliance is that it's one of the very few sports where you can imbibe with impunity during competition. In fact, a few swift ones may even help settle your nerves. *Just make sure you've completed the first hole before alcohol passes your lips.* (Chi Chi Rodríguez, the famous Puerto Rican pro from the 1960s and '70s claimed once to have downed a whole bottle of rum before teeing off at the Masters. "I shot the happiest 83 of my life," he said.)

This brings us on to the subject of beverage-cart girls. An increasingly common sight at golf clubs across the US, these essential but often underrated employees roam the courses in golf carts converted into mobile bars. They sell snacks, energy drinks, insect repellent, and lots and lots of beer—a simple yet vital service. Universally young and pretty, they offer lots of flirting but very little advice that might help your game. Some clubs go a step farther, offering young ladies who both caddy and serve drinks at the same time. And if it's an all-female golf party, then, in the interests of equality, some clubs offer beverage-cart boys, too.

But what if your club is devoid of cart girls/cart boys? (They're a pretty rare sight in Europe.) Can you bring along your own beers? It's okay for large groups in golf carts. If you're on foot, however, *you can hardly stuff cold beers in your golf bag. That would be uncouth.* Not to mention the fizz factor when you pop them open. That's the sort of thing John Daly might do, stopping behind a bush to shotgun a Bud after the front nine.

Modern golfers are more sophisticated than that. Golf is a gentleman's sport, like fly-fishing or grouse-shooting. ~~*Any booze you carry should be secreted in a hip flask.*~~ And it should be of the highest quality. Single malt keeps your handicap in single figures.

When it comes to the professional game, one golfer knows more about alcohol than anyone else. Yes, you guessed it again: John Daly. Although he's now on the wagon, his tales of previous alcoholic excess are legendary. For years he was obsessed with a guy known as Jack Daniels. "JD and JD were quite a pair—practically inseparable," he wrote in his biography *My Life In and Out of the Rough.* "Most people would be drunk for a month on what I'd had before dinner."

However, Jack Daniels wasn't a loyal friend to John Daly. There were the hospital visits to have his stomach pumped. There were the gargantuan gambling losses. There were the trashed hotel rooms, rock-and-roll style. And there was the time he passed out with his eyes open. "The guys I was drinking with thought I'd had a stroke or something. The next day I shot two under."

This boozy lifestyle culminated in a massive binge-drinking session in 2008, after which he was found passed out from alcohol and detained by police in North Carolina. The PGA suspended him for six months and apparently he's been teetotal ever since.

We're not condoning smoking, but *golf is a rare sport where a 20-a-day habit won't affect your score.* (It may kill you off before you're 40, but it won't increase your handicap.) The only problem is cigarette-butt etiquette. Where do you dispose of the ends?

In the bunkers, that's where. Think of these sand traps as giant ashtrays. Of course you can't simply go flicking your cigarette ends willy-nilly. *The proper way to extinguish them is to bend down and push the smoke deep into the sand* where the greenkeeper won't notice it—deep enough that only the most vigorous raking risks exhuming it. In three years it will biodegrade and no one—least of all the greenkeeper—will be any the wiser. Oh, and congratulate yourself that no wildfires have flared up on your account.

Chain smokers could do worse than play the Whistling Straits golf course in Kohler, Wisconsin. Its flagship Straits Course is reputed to have over 900 bunkers, some barely large enough to allow a golfer to swing the club. In fact, many of them are so small that they don't immediately look like bunkers. Pro player Dustin Johnson discovered this to his chagrin at the 2010 US PGA Championship when, on the final hole, he assumed his ball had landed on dusty ground. Grounding his club to play the shot as normal, he was then told that he was actually in a bunker and was duly awarded a two-shot penalty.

There are plenty of professional golfers who love a crafty smoke every now and then. Some of them even puff away while they're playing. The sport's poster boy for tobacco is Spaniard Miguel Ángel Jiménez, a veritable character who can often be spotted puffing on a fat cigar during practice rounds, while on the driving range, and at pro-am events. But, God forbid, never during competitive play. Now into his sixth decade and still winning, Jiménez was quizzed recently on the secrets of his longevity. "There is no secret," he said. "Good food, good wine, good cigars, and some exercise."

One player who is even less coy about his smoking habit is Argentina's Ángel Cabrera. He used to spark up happily while walking from one hole to the next. In recent years, probably as a sop to sponsors, he's stopped smoking during competitive play. But he puffs like a steam-train once the clubs are packed away.

And then there's John Daly, the man who has been addicted to pretty much everything at one time or another. On the subject of smoking during play, he has this to say: "I believe nicotine plus caffeine equals protein."

11 WINNER OF THE PREVIOUS HOLE DRIVES THE CART

Win the hole and you will, of course, be first to tee off on the following hole. Think about it, though. How much of a reward is that? Big deal. Shouldn't hole-victory earn you a more exciting privilege than the teeing honor? Such as *getting to be in charge of the golf cart*, for instance. Yes, *that's more like it*. Win the hole and you become designated cart driver, which of course means you get to park the cart nearest your ball once you've all teed off, saving yourself valuable calories.

Oh, and while we're on the subject of golf carts—*don't be too restricted about where you drive them.* In the old days you always had to stick to the cart paths. Nowadays, as long as you don't mount the greens or the tees, you can pretty much trundle where you want. Except for the bunkers, that is. This is golf, not the Dakar Rally, after all.

If you need a shining example of how NOT to practice golf-cart etiquette, then check out the stunts from the *Jackass* movies. In these highbrow docudramas, our intrepid heroes set out to road test golf carts to the very limit. Using a variety of golf courses, miniature golf courses, and waste grounds as their test beds, they perform the kind of gravity-defying motoring stunts you wouldn't think possible in a compact electric vehicle.

Even the New Rules of Golf would never tolerate shenanigans such as these. But, *should you win the hole and find yourself at the wheel, feel free to experiment with the golf cart's handling.* In the name of research, discover its top speed, its braking distance, its minimum turning circle, and the grip quality of its tires—just as long as you're suitably distant from the clubhouse. Perhaps draw short of trying to catch air like our friends from *Jackass*.

Murray gets lost in translation

One person who has experimented with golf-cart handling more than most is movie actor Bill Murray. In 2007, while in Sweden to play a pro-am tournament, he was stopped by police in the center of the Swedish capital at the wheel of a golf cart in the early hours of the morning. Stockholm's finest couldn't help noticing a strong aroma of alcohol.

"He refused to blow in the [breathalyzer] instrument, citing American legislation," the arresting officer later revealed. "So we applied the old method—a blood test."

Apparently, in Sweden, it's not illegal to drive a golf cart in traffic. It is unusual, however. "I have done this since 1968 and I've never experienced anything like this," the police officer added.

A few days later, Murray himself explained that he and some friends had driven to a tournament party in the golf cart. After the party had finished, no one had wanted to drive back home so Murray had done the chivalrous thing and offered his services as a chauffeur. "I ended up stopping and dropping people off on the way like a bus," he said. "I had about six people in the thing and I dropped them off one at a time." It was at the final stop, outside a 7-Eleven, that the police intervened. "They asked me to come over and assumed that I was drunk, and I tried to explain to them that I was a golfer."

Something, somewhere, obviously got lost in translation.

Sledging (or unwarranted verbal abuse of other players) is allowed in golf. In fact, it's to be encouraged. *Insulting your golfing partners is a sign of affection, of veiled respect. Plus, it will help you win.*

Golf sledging has been around longer than plus fours. The old favorites normally involve rubbing salt into the wounds. So, when a putt comes up short, try the following: "I'll give you $10 if you miss this next one, too." Or "Do you need some lead tape for your putter?"

Should your buddy tee off straight into the woods, try this: "You could wrap that up in juicy bacon and even Lassie wouldn't find it."

Comments suggesting your (male) partner might lack the appropriate gonads are perennial favorites, too: "Does your boyfriend play golf, too?" you might enquire after he shanks it off the tee into the bushes. "You just dropped your lipstick," you would say after he leaves an easy putt too short. Or "Did your purse get in the way?" after a basic putt goes wildly errant.

Casual sexism notwithstanding, the best sledges of all are those that mess with a player's brain: the old Jedi-mind tricks, the type of stuff that Yoda might come out with at his country club, on the other side of the galaxy. Here's a great example: just as your partner is about to tee off, subtly ask him if he breathes in or breathes out on his backswing. You can guarantee that's all he'll be thinking about for the rest of the round. Or, just as he's lining up for a crucial putt, casually inquire: "Do you always tuck your elbows in like that?" You can be certain he'll miss the cup.

Although not verbal, another way to put off a fellow player is to take a picture. Often otherwise competent golfers can turn into nervous wrecks as soon as a lens is pointed in their direction. Just ask Tiger Woods how he feels about being papped. At the 2014 British Open, held at Royal Liverpool Golf Club, the camera-shy Tiger lost his cool, roaring at a group of photographers hoping to get a decent snap of the star.

According to the New Rules of Golf, there's only one scenario when sledging is not permitted, and that's right at the point when your partner is taking his backswing. We do have some standards to maintain, after all.

13 HOLE IN ONE EQUALS MASSIVE BAR BILL

Everyone knows the loser of the round has to buy the beers at the 19th. That goes without saying. But in the New Rules of Golf there is a far greater forfeit than that. It comes about, should you be skilled enough (or fluky enough) to hit a hole in one. Once you get back to the club bar—by which time everyone will have been regaled with the story of your derring-do—*it's your honor-bound duty to buy a drink for everyone in the clubhouse*: the greenkeepers, the bar staff, the cleaning staff, the pet dog… Everyone. On the PGA Tour, where top pros earn thousands of dollars a minute, drinks for everyone ought to be mandatory. After all, pros are often gifted a free car when they shoot an ace. So a hefty bar bill is no major inconvenience.

In 2014, English golfer Andy Sullivan won a lot more than a free car when he holed an ace at the KLM Open in the Netherlands. You might say his prize was out of this world. Thanks to his 163-yard hole in one on the 15th, this European Tour player was given the chance to blast off into space. His reward, courtesy of Amsterdam-based XCOR Space Expeditions, was a short flight into space in a Lynx sub-orbital space plane, complete with a few minutes of zero gravity. (Not quite as good as *Apollo* astronaut Alan Shepard who, in 1971, hit a golf ball on the Moon, but impressive all the same.) Fellow European Tour golfer David Lynn later joked that if he'd won the space flight, he'd have given it to his caddy. "One way," he added.

If glamorous prizes such as these had been around in the 1970s, tournament sponsors would have been obliged to offer a lot more than a brief space flight to English player John Hudson. Competing in the 1971 Martini International, at the Royal Norwich Golf Club, he hit two aces, one straight after the other. First up was the par-3 195-yard 11th hole, guided gently in with a 4-iron. The next hole was 311 yards, par-4. This time, armed with a driver, he was in luck again. It's believed to be the only time a player has struck two consecutive holes in one in a professional tournament. That little feat surely ought to have earned him a trip to the Moon.

PATHETIC EXCUSES ARE PERFECTLY ACCEPTABLE

Some days you can't play for toffee. You top it, you whiff it, you shank it, and you spend more time hacking through the rough than you do ambling down the fairways. But remember—*bad golf is never your fault.* The New Rules of Golf allow you to *blame your pitifully poor play on anything you like, as long as it's not your good self.*

The weather is always a suitable scapegoat. "The goddamn wind changed on my backswing," you should say, spitting with venom, as your tee shots fly off into the forest. "That putt would have gone in a week ago! Cursed rain!" you yell as your ball goes three feet wide for a quadruple bogey. "The sun was in my eyes," you moan as your approach shot loops in a perfect parabola right into the lake.

There's nothing wrong with questioning the skills of the greenkeepers, either. "There's too much/not enough sand in the bunkers!" "These greens are nothing like the practice greens!" "The ball must have bounced off a stone." Or the simple yet classic, "These greens are shit!" (Mention that they are riddled with a certain obscure species of invasive Asian weed and you will sound more convincing. If you can use the weed's Latin name, all the better.)

But some days the weather and the course are just too perfect. In which case, like the proverbial bad workman, you must *blame your tools.* "I just can't get the hang of this new putter." "My dog chewed my glove, and the slobber made my hand slip." "My ball had mud on it."

Even the pros have to be inventive with their excuses. In 2013, Rory McIlroy abandoned the Honda Classic in Florida halfway through, citing pain in his wisdom teeth. "I sincerely apologize," he said in a statement afterwards. "I have been suffering with a sore wisdom tooth, which is due to come out in the near future. It began bothering me again last night, so I relieved it with Advil. It was very painful again this morning, and I was simply unable to concentrate. It was really bothering me and had begun to affect my playing partners."

Let's hope the tooth fairy made poor little Rory's suffering worthwhile.

15 CELLPHONE ETIQUETTE

There used to be a time when cellphones were about as welcome at golf courses as Japanese knotweed. Nowadays, of course, they are ubiquitous. But that doesn't mean you can use them any time you like. Come on, golf time is sacred time. Answering calls (work or private) and checking e-mails is strictly prohibited. In fact, *there are only three scenarios where cellphone-use is permitted:*

1. It's your pregnant wife calling and she's almost full term. Even if her waters have broken and the baby's head is emerging, you must still, according to the New Rules, complete the hole and then mark double bogeys for any remaining holes on your round.

2. There's a major professional tournament on and you have big money riding on it. If you're spread betting, it may be necessary to check the in-play odds.

3. You need to film your buddy's short putts (see rule no. 17).

Forcing players to putt out really short putts is churlish. *Normal etiquette states anything within a trashcan lid's diameter from the cup is a gimme.*

The New Rules of Golf are even more flexible on this. Slightly more than a trashcan lid is fine. We're all grown-ups here, right? Just as long as you remember that it's a domestic trashcan lid. Once you start getting into wheelie bin or dumpster territory, you're being too generous.

There are two exceptions to the gimme rule when you're perfectly entitled to force your partner to play the putt:

1. If there's money on the game.

2. If you think your partner's putt might make for a good video opportunity (see rule no. 17).

17 ALWAYS VIDEO YOUR PARTNER'S REALLY SHORT PUTTS

Social media has done wonders for the sport of golf. It's given us the Twitter ramblings of Ian Poulter, Rickie Fowler, and, perhaps most impressive of all, Jason Dufner. It's given us @GolfClubWanker. It's allowed us to *watch, and re-watch, Tiger Woods losing his temper as photographers click their shutters on his backswing.*

One area where amateurs, too, can maximize their social media presence is by filming their partner's short putts on their smartphones and then, provided the result is suitably embarrassing, posting it on YouTube. *Pretty much anything between three feet and five feet should be committed to celluloid in the hope that disaster will ensue.* (If you're really determined to humiliate your buddy, you might renege on the gimme rule and insist that he plays putts under three feet, too.)

You know the scenario: your partner has just spent three minutes lining up an easy three-footer. Nice, gentle grip; smooth, easy backswing; focused and determined; then, just at the last minute, he takes his eye off the ball and it horseshoes round the edge of the cup, back towards him. Immediately, like the director of a Hollywood action flick, you must now turn your camera to focus on your buddy's facial reactions. *That's what your viewers all want to see: his frustration, his humiliation, his utter dejection.*

That's certainly the case with the pro tours. There's nothing more entertaining than seeing a world-class golfer miss a short putt at the business end of a tournament—even better if that putt could have won them the championship. The classic example is Scott Hoch at the 1989 Masters. In a sudden-death play-off with Nick Faldo, all Hoch needed for outright victory and the right to don the famous green jacket was an easy two-foot putt. It turned out to be an unforgettable defeat snatched from the jaws of victory. He pulled the shot entirely. The ball didn't even hit the edge of the cup.

"I looked at my par putt to win, and I had a good idea of what it was going to do and how I wanted to hit it," Hoch remembered long after this disastrous episode. "I was behind it, and I started to go to address it. [But] I didn't have the thoughts I wanted to. I was thinking of other things like, 'Okay, finally I'm going to win a major,' instead of thinking about the putt." Then Hoch made his fatal mistake. He stepped back from the putt to look at it once more. "To get my mind straight," he said.

What he was actually doing was choking big time. After finally making his play, he pulled it wide of the cup. He'd blown the Masters.

Next, the two players moved on to the par-4 11th where Faldo sunk a superb 30-foot birdie to take victory. "I'm glad I don't carry a gun," the loser said afterwards. For years he was known as "Hoch the Choke."

To this day, however, the American player remains stoical. "How much will the putt define my legacy?" he asks. "I don't know. I try to justify it by thinking: 'Hey, if I had won a major, I could have gotten in a plane crash trying to chase money somewhere.' Things could have happened to me that weren't good. I just look at it as a chance missed."

Indeed.

When playing solo, there's nothing wrong with wearing headphones and listening to tunes out on the course. *It's been scientifically proven that music increases one's sporting performance.* Apparently it tricks your mind into feeling less tired after physical effort, and it encourages positive thoughts. Of course, different types of music will help different golfers. One man's Mozart is another man's Metallica.

Unfortunately, there hasn't been a single decent song penned about our wonderful sport. Bing Crosby's appalling 1957 hit "Straight Down the Middle" is probably the most famous golf song, while most other tend to be novelty offerings. There's the unfathomably bad "The Golf Song" by Arrogant Worms. ("I just hope I clear the ladies tee/ Everybody hits it farther than me/ Just eight more strokes then I reach a par-3.") Then there's a hip-hop number called "Golf Boys" by Golf Boys. "I like olives in my Rory Sabbatini," they rap. "One time I got asked to play in a bikini/ Said it was for a really good cause/ I thought about it then I said Kevin Na!" There's even a golf-themed country singer by the name of Golf Brooks. Only marginally better is Dave Loggins' "Augusta," a vocal version of the theme song from The Masters broadcasts.

Worst of all, however, must be a whole album of golf-themed songs called *Great Golf Hits, Volume 1*, compiled by a teaching pro called Stan Buzas. It includes parodies of the likes of Rod Stewart, Tina Turner, Queen, ELO, The Police, and Tom Petty. The song titles tell you all you need to know: "Some Guys Make All The Putts," "What's Clubs Got To Do With It?," "Hit Me On The Sweet Spot."

To get inspired on the course, you're going to need far better tunes than these. Crank up the volume. Just don't then moan should you get struck by another player's ball. *Remember: when you're rocking, you can't hear "Fore!"*

19 BE PROUD OF YOUR HOME CLUB

You know how some clubs insist you sign the visitors' book before you play on their course as a guest? Often they'll request you write down your handicap, plus the name of your home club.

However downscale that home club may be, always be proud of it. Sign its name in the book. Saying that, there's nothing wrong with being a little bit creative with the name. If the Los Angeles Municipal or the Central London Golf Centre don't sound posh enough, then *feel free to embellish them with an upscale prefix or suffix*:

The Los Angeles Municipal Country Club, for example, or The Royal Central London Golf Centre.

ROYAL
ST CRAZY'S
GOLF COURSE

What if you're not a golf club member at all? Well, *if the club you're visiting has the audacity to attempt to shame you, then you have every right to have the audacity to invent a fictitious golf club* and write it down in the visitors' book. Just choose a very ordinary (the more ordinary the better) town near where you live and add your upscale prefix or suffix. However stuffy the club manager, he'll never dare question the existence of the Royal and Ancient Peckham or the Bronx Golf and Country Club.

DON'T BE A BANDIT 20

No one likes a bandit. (Otherwise known as a sandbagger.) The New Rules of Golf of course frown upon any attempt artificially *to inflate one's handicap in order to win bets. It's tantamount to defecating in the bunker on the 18th.*

Yet it happens a lot. As soon as there's money on a game, there's always someone, somewhere, who thinks he can lie about his real handicap. He plays to a five but actually carries a ten. Stop it! Be honest. *You're cheating your friends AND yourself.*

There's a punishment for any golfer found to be indulging in banditry: he must spend the rest of the day sulking beneath a large, Mexican sombrero, thinking about the error of his ways.

Our wonderful sport has given rise to some highly inventive slang terms. The New Rules of Golf require you to *use these terms liberally and always in a suitably derisive tone.*

A Lance Armstrong: you've lost your ball so you start cheating

An Anna Kournikova: it looked great, but won't win any prizes

Army golf: your first shot goes left, your second shot right, your third shot left; left, right, left, right…

A Cuban: a putt that stops just millimeters short of the hole, i.e. it needs one more revolution

A Saddam Hussein: going from bunker to bunker

A Princess Di: shouldn't have used a driver

A Rock Hudson: thought it was straight but it wasn't

A Justin Bieber: you want to smack it really hard, but you'll probably get into trouble if you do

A Joe Pesci: a nasty little five-footer

A Hitler: two shots in the bunker

A condom shot: it's safe, but really didn't feel very good

An O.J. Simpson: it was risky but somehow you got away with it

A Pharaoh: buried in the sand

A Bin Laden: driven into the hills, never to be seen again

A son-in-law: not exactly what you wanted but it'll have to do

A Mick Jagger: a big lip out

A Ryanair: it flew okay, but landed miles from the destination you wanted

OFFER TO LET THE GROUP BEHIND OVERTAKE

Yes, courses can get congested, but if your group is playing slowly, you must let faster groups overtake. The New Rules say that if you're more than five holes into the round and you see the group behind you kicking their heels on the tee, then *wave them through*. The issue is a group behind will never ask to play through because it's considered rude. So what happens is that they end up dropping subtle (or not so subtle) hints by hitting balls right up to the back of your heels. And that can be intimidating for the slower group. This rule sidesteps the problem.

PEE STOPS ARE OKAY DURING BALL SEARCHES

Searching for errant balls is tedious, but The New Rules state you must always help unfortunate members of your group who have lost a ball in the woods. It's the gentlemanly thing to do. But see it as a potential comfort break, too. After five minutes of thrashing through the bushes to no avail, there's nothing wrong with everyone having a communal pee stop. *If nature has called for one's ball, it's perfectly entitled to call for one's bladder*. And, at the same time, you're perfectly entitled to relieve yourself. Just make sure you don't accidentally hydrate your partner's lost ball in the process.

Chapter Three
The New Rules of Golf Equipment

Yes, we all know Tiger Woods has a fluffy tiger on his driver. *But he's Tiger Woods. You are not. And for that reason you are not permitted a novelty head cover.* It is invariably uncool.

Not that Tiger's head cover is cool. Apparently his mother knitted it for him. The words "Love from Mom" in Thai (his mother's native language) are stitched upon it. *This man has won multiple majors and he still feels the need for a fluffy mascot from mommy.*

Ian Poulter has a selfie head cover, which is not only uncool but exceedingly vain. Added to that, it doesn't resemble the man in the slightest. It looks more like Statler or Waldorf, the two grumpy old men from The Muppets.

Sergio García has fluffy bulls as his head covers, universal symbols for Spanish power… and cruelty to animals. Richard Green sports a wallaby in homage to his native Australia. Tim Clark has a penguin called Henry. John Daly has a lion.

As an amateur you should strive to be much cooler than these guys. Novelty head covers do not improve your golf. Almost as bad are ones that profess loyalty to your favorite sports team. Cocooning your woods in a Manchester United or a New York Yankees cover is not the way to do it. Yes, you need to protect your expensive weapons, but, in the name of good taste, do it with plain head covers.

25 NEVER MIX YOUR BRANDS OF IRON

A TaylorMade driver, a Titleist wedge, an Odyssey putter. No problem about mixing the brands in your bag. But *whatever you do, don't mix your medium irons. These bad boys must be all the same brand.*

It looks slovenly if your irons are from multiple manufacturers—as if you've picked them up, here and there, over the years, from various thrift shops. There's also a practical reason for homogeneity: *if they're of the same brand and the same range, then it follows that they will have similar weight distribution and similar styles of play.* This will help you get some sort of consistency in your play. Common sense.

44

Range-finder binoculars are illegal in competitive golf. They are also illegal according to the New Rules of Golf. That's because, essentially, they're a waste of space. (Plus *they make you look like a reject from the special forces.*) Use your course guide and you'll have more than enough information to gauge the distance of your shot. Yes, binoculars are more precise, but just how precise does an amateur need to be? The course guide tells you it's a 170-yard approach to the pin. Your range finder tells you it's actually 172 yards—as if you were going to change your technique and swap your club, just for those two extra yards. Get real! You're going to stick to the club selected and aim for the middle of the green. Rely too much on range finders and you quickly lose your ability to gauge distances when you're in competition. (Plus, they're anti-social since they're so fiddly to use). *One of the many challenges of golf is judging how far you need to hit the ball.*

A golfer with binoculars is like an orienteer runner with a GPS. It's called cheating.

For the very same reason, don't buy yourself a GPS watch. In this world of high-tech gadgets, *it's good to go old school every now and then.*

DON'T ARRANGE YOUR CLUBS IN THE CORRECT ORDER

Anally retentive golfers will tell you a well-ordered golf bag is crucial, that it allows you to select the correct club quickly, that it keeps the bag balanced while you carry it. What a crock. What an utter waste of time. *Worrying about the order of your clubs won't help your game in the slightest. If anything, it will use up valuable mental energy.*

It's not like you can't distinguish the correct club when you need it. Ordering your clubs is a bit like arranging the bottles of beer on your refrigerator shelf according to brand, size, and strength. Stop worrying and just drink them.

In fact, the only reason to separate any of your clubs is *if you have an expensive putter. Place it with the woods rather than letting it rattle around with the irons where it might get dented.* And apply all that excess mental energy to your game instead.

CLUBS MUST NOT COST MORE THAN THE CAR THEY LIVE IN

The New Rules of Golf are quite clear on this point. There's something seriously wrong with you if the clubs in your trunk are worth more than the car you drive.

There's nothing wrong with spending a month's salary on a new set of clubs (see rule no. 30), but only if you've already spent at least a couple of months' wages on your motor. Get your priorities straight. The opposite sex is more impressed by a Maserati than by expensive golf clubs.

NOTHING WRONG WITH A HALF SET OF CLUBS

Use brainpower rather than back power. On practice rounds, or nine-hole golf courses, you simply don't require all 14 clubs. Instead, carry a half set and store it in a slim-line pencil bag.

Unless you're seriously competing, you only need eight clubs, nine at a push. Arm yourself with your driver, your hybrid, your 5-, 7-, and 9-irons, your pitching wedge, your sand wedge, and your putter. Leave your 3-wood, your 5-wood, and your remaining irons in the car. For just nine holes, or practice rounds, they are surplus to requirements. And, if you're walking the course, your back will appreciate the lighter weight.

A club too many

On the subject of surplus clubs, do you remember what happened to British golfer Ian Woosnam at the 2001 Open Championship? After starting his round beautifully at the Royal Lytham & St Annes Golf Club in Lancashire, UK, with a birdie on the first, he stepped up confidently to the second tee, ready to take on the world.

But the world wasn't having it. Suddenly his caddie uttered seven words that will no doubt haunt the Welshman for the rest of his life: "We've got two drivers in the bag."

Give Woosnam his due. He immediately fessed up. Knowing that players are permitted only 14 clubs, he first flung the offending club (a second driver he had been trying out on the practice range) into the rough. He then told the match referee of his error and was duly handed a two-stroke penalty.

Much worse, though, was the effect the whole sorry incident had on the player's composure. "God! I give you a job to do and you can't do it," he growled at his mortified caddie Miles Byrne, whose responsibility it was, of course, to ensure only 14 clubs were in his player's bag. From Woosnam's body language, it was obvious he played the rest of the round in something of a silent rage. He ended up tying for third.

Only weeks later Woosnam and Byrne parted company. Not surprising, really, seeing that the infamous 15th club cost the player over £218,000 in prize money and a potential spot in Europe's Ryder Cup team.

Time to buy a new set of golf clubs? *If you're serious about your game, then you really should think about investing in custom-fitted clubs.* Yes, they're a lot more expensive, but they're well worth it.

The manufacturer will measure your height, the distance from wrist to floor, your glove size, and various other areas of your anatomy. Then they'll analyze your swing technique—your face angle, launch angle, attack angle, ball speed, spin rate, and club path—before feeding you the old cliché about your "swing being as unique as your fingerprint." But the new (and expensive) weapons you walk away with will definitely help your game—at least to a certain extent.

Come on. Live a little. *You wouldn't buy a suit off the Internet. So have a bit of self-respect when you buy your new clubs.*

And if that means you need to wash them in the kitchen sink on a Saturday afternoon, well so be it. When it's wet and rainy, your clubs are going to get covered in mud and grass. *Gently wash them in the sink with a soft sponge before drying them off with a fluffy white towel. You're not a real golfer until you've done this (and been severely reprimanded).*

It's only common sense to keep your treasured clubs pristine. After all, you wouldn't buy an expensive suit or car and not get it cleaned or valeted.

Not all of us are fortunate enough to play our golf in sunny climes. In many parts of the world a good, strong umbrella is just as essential as a decent putter. But *make sure it's a golf-specific umbrella rather than one of those flimsy pop-ups* you see Japanese tourists gadding about town with.

Golf-specific doesn't mean it has to be from an expensive manufacturer, however. Any brand will do. After all, they're all made in the same factories. Just check the quality before you buy. Be sure the stretchers and ribs are solid and made of metal and that the tips will stay in place, however strong a gale is blowing. Don't buy one with a flimsy tube or spring mechanism. *Cowering from a rain shower, halfway through the back nine, you'll be mighty glad you invested in a decent one.*

Alternatively, you could follow the advice of Texan golfer, and winner of six majors, Lee Trevino. At the 1975 Western Open in Illinois, he was struck by a bolt of lightning that entered through his bag, up his arm, and into his back. "I should have held up a 1-iron," he quipped afterwards. "Not even God can hit a 1-iron." Fortunately, back surgery to alleviate the pain from the electrocution allowed him to play on through a glittering career.

South Africa's Retief Goosen is another top-level golfer who knows all too well the power of electrical storms. In the mid-1980s, playing an amateur tournament in South Africa, he was struck by a bolt that left him with reduced hearing and an irregular heartbeat. His golf outfit was severely burnt. Apparently, to this day, he keeps it as a souvenir.

Exposed as they are, in open countryside and brandishing metal rods, golfers are human lightning conductors. Worldwide, dozens are killed every year. Take the case of 45-year-old John Needham, who was playing an amateur match at the Inniscrone Golf Club, in Pennsylvania, in 2005. Halfway through the seventh hole he was struck by a vicious lightning bolt and collapsed in a heap on the ground, stone dead. The heat of the strike was so intense that the gold chain around his neck melted and stuck to the skin of his corpse.

"Around here, we have a saying: Everyone has a lifetime clock," said Buford Wilcox, who was one of Needham's foursome that fateful day. "It doesn't matter what you're doing or where you are. When your time comes up, death is going to get you. Even on the seventh fairway."

GOLFING GADGETS

Ever heard of the UroClub? "A camouflaged portable urinal, designed to be discreet, sanitary, and create an air of privacy," says the sales spiel. "It looks like an ordinary golf club and comes equipped with a unique removable golf towel clipped to the shaft that functions as a privacy shield. Imagine, giving the appearance of taking a practice swing, while both privately and confidentially, you are able to relieve yourself without any

embarrassment. Have the confidence to drink whatever you wish during your game and not worry if you'll make it to the clubhouse in time."

We joke not. This is a genuine golfing product, invented by a certified urologist, and sold as "the only club in your bag guaranteed to keep you out of the woods." We're sure it works perfectly and has years of research behind it. But it's a gadget you really don't need to be spending your hard-earned cash on. If you need a pee, nip into the bushes.

Our glorious sport is littered with gadgets such as this that claim to give your game an edge. Straitjackets that perfect your swing; sensors that clip to your glove and then beam your swing analysis to your smart phone; gyroscopes that keep your clubs level; golf-bag alarms; golf-ball-finder glasses; the toilet putting green: for golfers who want to be No.1 while doing a No.1.

Well, here's some news for you. *The New Rules of Golf prohibit you from ever buying a tacky golfing gadget.* Especially one that allows you to urinate into a fake golf club.

ALWAYS TAKE YOUR OWN CLUBS ON VACATION

34

It can cost a hell of a lot of money to take your clubs with you on an airplane—on some of Europe's cheaper airlines it's sometimes more than the cost of the flight itself. But *when you arrive at your golf resort and find yourself perusing the filthy, scuffed, and dented rental clubs on offer, you quickly realize it's all worth it.*

And if you're worried about those cavalier baggage handlers at the airport, then invest in a padded flight bag for your clubs. Otherwise they could well end up in just as sorry a state as the resort's rental ones.

Cart-path-only courses are bad news. Aesthetically, they spoil the grand, sweeping curves of a well-designed course. Tactically, more than once, you'll find yourself cursing as your tee shot lands on the path and bounces farther into the rough. But at least, *once you're out of sight of the clubhouse, you can happily drive where you like. Right? Actually, not if your cart has a special GPS device installed.* On some courses these devices cause the vehicle's engine to cut out when you stray too far off the path.

It's a blight on modern golf. If you smack your ball wildly, you're going to want to get in the cart and go after it. Even if that does mean driving through the rough. *So stand up for your rights and boycott any cart that cuts out when you go off-road.*

Nearly all golf carts also have speed governors installed. There's a way to get round this killjoy device, however. And on some carts it's as simple as bending a cable. Have a look on YouTube for instructions and then happily put your pedal to the metal.

One golf course where you need more than a speedy golf cart is the Legend Golf & Safari Resort, in South Africa's Limpopo Province. Here there is a hole called the Extreme 19th, arguably the most difficult golf hole on the planet. To access the tee, 1,300 feet up, on top of Hangklip Mountain, you need a helicopter. Once you tee off, it takes around 20 seconds for the ball to drop onto the fairway below. Cameras and human spotters are used to follow the track of the balls as players attempt to land them on the green, which has the shape of the African continent, along with contours that mimic its mountain ranges. This is not an easy hole. At the time of writing, no one had ever achieved a hole in one, however, the course owners promise that should anyone do so, they "will make him/her famous."

On all par-3 holes you must locate a discarded, broken tee and use it for your tee shot. For such a short hole you'll be using an iron anyway, so the ball doesn't need to sit up high. There's the bonus that you'll be recycling a small piece of wood, thereby reducing your carbon footprint. Plus you'll be saving the greenkeeper time on litter duty. *And don't let any rule-Nazi tell you that using a discarded tee constitutes "using someone else's equipment," thereby resulting in a penalty. It's perfectly acceptable within the official rules of golf.*

While we're on the subject of tees, it won't surprise you to learn that the New Rules of Golf are very forthright *when it comes to novelty tees. You are not permitted, under any circumstances, to employ these horrible little items.* You know the sort: nude lady tees (aka "strip tees"), nude man tees, celebrity tees, smiley-face tees, tees with cheesy messages printed on them. If you ever see someone using one, immediately confiscate it, build a little campfire in a bunker, and ceremoniously cremate it.

English golfer Ian Poulter was once spotted using tees adorned with the logo of his favorite soccer club, Arsenal. Unforgivable.

ELECTRIC GOLF-TROLLEYS ARE TOE-CURLINGLY AWFUL

All the electric golf trolleys on planet Earth should be rounded up onto the world's biggest links course and then—using remote controls—driven like lemmings off a very high cliff into the sea. Never to be seen again.

Electric golf trolleys are an abomination. Anyone who ever uses one should be dumped headfirst, stark naked inside one and paraded through the streets of his home town.

Golf Segways are even more abominable. Offenders will receive a severe beating with a 9-iron before being expelled from their club for evermore.

Get the message?

You know the type. They turn up for a foursome, wearing an obnoxiously colorful pair of golf pants (see rule no. 45), and, with a magician's flourish, from the depths of their bag, they produce a ball on which they have had printed both their name and some witty message. Something side-splittingly hilarious such as "Hands off my balls!" "Drive for show, putt for dough," "It takes balls to play like me," "Golf is better than sex," "Hole in one," or "Tee-rific!" Aaaaaaagh!

Birthday greetings, wedding messages, happy anniversaries, and other greetings are equally banned. In fact, the New Rules of Golf ban all such customized balls in the name of good taste.

Even the pros can't help themselves sometimes, getting their balls monogrammed or other such nonsense. In a display of utter vanity, Japanese player Ryo Ishikawa has his balls embellished with a cartoon image of his head. (Mind you, his nickname is "The Bashful Prince.") If you're ever spectating at a tournament where he's competing and his ball lands anywhere near you, then you're perfectly entitled to pocket it as a souvenir. Perhaps it will encourage him to repent.

And should you ever find yourself tempted to spend your own hard-earned cash on such a ridiculous novelty... Stop! Spend it on buying higher-quality golf balls instead.

Apparently even President Obama has his golf balls monogrammed. In 2014, while playing at the Congressional Country Club course in

Maryland, he must have shanked one of them into the woods because, a day later, a local player exhumed said ball from the undergrowth, took a photo of it, and posted it on Twitter. On one side was etched the number 44 (as in the 44th president of the United States), on the other was the acronym POTUS.

Actually, come to think of it, that's pretty cool. *The New Rules of Golf hereby officially exempt Barack Obama from the ban on self-printed balls. But only him.*

Long putters are soon to be consigned to history. (Thank God.) *From January 2016, competitive players will no longer be allowed to play an anchored stroke*—when the club or the gripping hand is intentionally held against the body to create a hinge effect.

Not all pro golfers are happy. Adam Scott won the 2013 Masters with anchored putts. In 2012, Ernie Els and Webb Simpson employed the technique to take victory in the British Open and US Open, respectively. Keegan Bradley won the 2011 PGA Championship thanks to a spot of anchoring. Carl Pettersson, who's rather keen on long putters, too, called the ban "a witch hunt." But none of this changes the fact that *long, anchored putters look unmitigatedly dorky.* Anchoring is for sailors, not golfers. This new rule—Rule 14-1b—is great news for all right-minded players. It should be embraced. Long live Rule 14-1b! *Death to the long putters!*

There are two bold reasons why anchored putting had to go. First of all, it gave players an unfair advantage. Both major governing bodies (the R&A and the United States Golf Association) agree. Glen Nager is president of the latter. "Anchoring creates potential advantages," he said, "such as making the stroke simpler and more repeatable, restricting the movement and rotation of the hands, arms, and clubface, creating a fixed pivot point, and creating extra support and stability that may diminish the effects of nerves and pressure."

Secondly, anchored putters—either the broomstick variety or the belly models—look really uncool. Especially the belly putters when they're pushed up into the protruding gut of a middle-aged golfer. Colin Montgomerie, who knows a thing or two about protruding guts, once admitted: "I wouldn't have holed the winning putt at the 2004 Ryder Cup if I had not been using a belly putter." What he forgot to add was: "I wouldn't have looked like a total dork if I hadn't used a belly putter."

Rule 14-1b does not ban long putters per se, just the anchoring of them to your body, which means *golfers are free to continue using long putters as long as they swing them clear of their protruding guts.*

This is where the New Rules of Golf (that other famous governing body for golf) must step in. Not only does it ban the use of anchored putters, but it bans all long putters altogether. *Get with the program. Get a normal putter.* If you really feel the need to go off piste, then take a leaf out of Happy Gilmore's book and putt with a hockey stick.

The final word on the subject must go to Tiger Woods: "I just believe the art of putting is swinging the club and controlling nerves. We swing all other 13 clubs. I think the putter should be the same."

This is golf. Not professional soccer. Not NBA basketball. And certainly not *Keeping Up with the Kardashians*. The New Rules of Golf do not allow players to be too showy on the course. That means no bling and no flashy accessories.

Under no circumstances may you pimp your golfing equipment.

In the professional game, Ian Poulter is a particular culprit in this department. He owns a platinum-diamond ball marker, for example, which should never be allowed. In 2011, at the World Matchplay in Spain, he almost got his just deserts when the tasteless object was momentarily lost on the course. Attempting to play his ball out of deep gorse, his right leg buckled, and he collapsed in a heap on the ground. That's when the glitzy ball marker must have slipped out of his pocket. Unfortunately the incident was picked up on the television replay, allowing officials later to retrieve the piece of jewelry. Far better if it had been lost forever.

Other bling golfing accessories banned by the New Rules of Golf include tees, divot replacers, or multi-tools made of precious metals. *Clubs featuring either gold, platinum, or precious gems are disgusting.* Any golf-themed jewelry is also prohibited.

Any time it looks like the weather might misbehave, make sure you pack waterproof pants and a jacket in your golf bag. There's one brand of waterproof suit that's head and shoulders above all others, and that's Galvin Green. You could happily pour a hose over it all day and you'd remain dry underneath. You could even play in Wales.

It was in Wales, at the 2010 Ryder Cup, that the entire Team USA learned the true meaning of waterproof. More water, less proof, to be exact. Perhaps they had underestimated the intensity of British rain. On the opening day of play they all got soaked to the skin. "Disappointing," was how they described their official team waterproofs. So disappointing, in fact, that the US captain Corey Pavin decided to blow £4,000 ($6,500) at the official store, splashing out on brand-new rain gear for his entire team. After all, *a dry team is a happy team.*

The European players were understandably delighted at their opponents' discomfort. "Our team room is happier than theirs right now," said Team Europe captain Colin Montgomerie. Ian Poulter added gloatingly: "Our [waterproofs] are keeping us nice and dry."

Some American commentators still refer to the incident as golf's very own "Water-gate."

Chapter Four
The New Rules of Golf Clothing

Pleats, turn-ups, crisply pressed seams straight from the dry cleaners. No guesses for what the New Rules of Golf say about these features on short pants. The thing about golf shorts is that you *wear them when it's scorching hot, and you like the idea of a leisurely, casual round.* Nothing too strenuous. Golf shorts shouldn't try too hard. If you're going to the bother of pleats, turn-ups, and pressed seams, then you're not going to be in the right mindset for a casual round of golf. Wear long pants instead.

If the New Rules of Golf had any sway over the PGA, then they would of course allow players to wear short pants. They're permitted in LPGA tournaments. Caddies are allowed to wear them. So why not the PGA players? In the name of sexual equality, *it's high time male pros were allowed to show off their legs.* (And not just when they've rolled up their pants to go fishing for balls in the water hazards.)

Granted, some players would look a lot better in shorts than others. At half mast, Tiger Woods, Rickie Fowler, and Adam Scott would turn a few heads. John Daly, Kevin Stadler, and Mark Calcavecchia, on the other hand, might turn a few stomachs.

TAN LINES ON YOUR LEGS ARE A NO-NO

While cyclists consider dead-straight tan lines on the biceps and thighs to be really cool, golfers do not. The New Rules of Golf state that *you should be able to strut proudly along the beach in your swimming shorts without betraying the fact you are a golfer*. To achieve this, you'll need a varied golfing wardrobe with shorts and shirts of different lengths. Or a spray-on tan.

Alternatively, golf clubs could officially designate one day a week as topless golf day. Men would be allowed to play with their shirts off while women could strip down to a sports bra. It would give all members the chance to top up their tans without worrying about tan lines.

Topless Tuesdays. That has a certain ring to it, don't you think?

THE SOCK RULE (44)

The days of having to wear knee-length socks with your shorts are thankfully long gone. *Knee-length socks are now only permissible if you're a cheerleader, a professional marathon runner, or a medieval Scotsman going into battle.* There are only two styles of socks permitted for golfers: low-cut ankle socks if you're wearing shorts and normal-length socks if you're wearing pants.

Some pretty unforgivable sock crimes have been committed on the LPGA Tour. Paula Creamer, with her red-and-white striped thigh highs, has raised a few eyebrows among the fashion police. Other female players fond of long, brightly-colored stockings include Michelle Wie, Ai Miyazato, Mika Miyazato, and Maria Hjorth.

And while we're in sock territory, it may as well be known that, aside from plain, dark colors, only one other pattern is allowed: argyle—but not any old argyle. Make sure it matches your shirt, or your pants, or your bag, or your golf cart… or something.

When it comes to golf pants, it's time to go Nordic. All the coolest designs come out of Scandinavia. Take J. Lindeberg or Oscar Jacobson. You won't find their pants covered in disgraceful 1980s-style pleats or turn-ups. You won't see dodgy buttons or flared ankles. If they come in a tartan pattern, it will be a cool tartan pattern. Not the sort of Braveheart kitsch you see Ian Poulter wearing.

There's a reason Scandinavian designs look so cool. Those Nordic cats are taller than the rest of us, which means the fashion designers generally opt for longer sleeves and longer legs. This makes even chubby golfers look slimmer. Flat-fronted jean-style pockets add to the effect.

Johan Lindeberg's designs have been revolutionary for golf. Back in the late 1990s, when he first burst onto the scene, he took the traditional golfing look, dragged it round the back of the clubhouse, and gave it a damn good thrashing.

"There are just so many terrible things in golf," he famously said. "It used to be so stylish but then something happened in the 1980s, which killed it all. It got into a trap, a 1980s trap, where for some reason the country look came in and then never went away. It is time it changed. Things have to change."

In the intervening years, things really have changed. Nowadays, many of the world's coolest golfers, wherever they happen to hail from, veer towards that slimmed-down Scandi-look. Adam Scott is the perfect example. Ryo Ishikawa, Martin Kaymer, and Rory McIlroy deserve honorable mentions, too. And don't forget the Scandinavians themselves.

Aware of his mighty influence on the aesthetics of golf, Lindeberg emphasizes how his brand is all about "fashionable taste, a rock-and-roll ethos, and a passion for golf." The New Rules of Golf applaud him.

Far away on the opposite side of the sartorial divide are professional golf's fashion faux pas. Poulter has already been picked out as a particular culprit. But even worse is Rickie Fowler. Snappily dressed most of the time, on the last day of each tournament he loves dressing up in an unforgivably awful all-orange outfit. Apparently it's in honor of his old alma mater, Oklahoma State University. He's lucky not to end up in Guantanamo Bay sporting that little number.

Who's the worst of the lot, though? There is one player on the PGA Tour whose taste in clothing is vomit-inducing, to say the least: John Daly. *With his fluorescent shirts and psychedelic trousers, he looks like a deranged clown on drugs*, or a visually-impaired kids' TV presenter. Watch him play for more than 10 minutes and you'll find yourself reaching for the headache pills. The New Rules of Golf would have Daly thrown out of the clubhouse instantly for severe crimes against fashion.

46   WEAR SHIRTS THAT WICK

On warm days, gray, beige, or pastel-colored shirts aren't a good look. *After nine holes, with the sun beating down on you, sweat patches will soon be blossoming under the armpits. Wet man-boobs are even worse.*

The answer, of course, is to opt for golf shirts in either white or very dark colors, made of a material that wicks. The quicker the wicker, the quicker it will dry. And you really want to be sure it's dry before you lean up against the spike bar at the end of your round. Look at Northern Irish pro Darren Clarke, for example. Although he's lost a phenomenal amount of weight, he's still quite efficient in the perspiration department, to say the least. Dark shirts suit him best.

The same goes for pants. *Old-school beige chinos don't suit hot climes.* Just ask PGA pro Robert Garrigus. Someone needs to confiscate all his beige pants.

Ideally you want your golf shirt to look fashionable enough so you can wear it proudly out to dinner after your round. More Tiger Woods than John Daly, in other words.

But even Daly's luminous shirts pale into insignificance compared to the fashion crime committed by Ian Poulter in 2006 at the Abu Dhabi Golf Championship, when he decided to wear the jersey of his favorite soccer team, Arsenal. This plummeted him to new depths and had the golf fashion police spitting blood. He was also very lucky not to get fined by the European Tour. It wasn't crimes against fashion they were worried about, but the oversized logo of the soccer club's sponsor. "It was just a bit of fun and I didn't mean to upset anybody," a contrite Poulter said afterwards. "I can't see any problem with the shirt. It has a collar and I am not being paid to wear it, nor do I have a contract to wear it. Yes, it has got an Arsenal club badge, and, yes, it does have the sponsorship, but I am not reaping any reward from it. At the moment I don't have a clothing contract and can wear whatever I want."

No you can't, Ian. The New Rules of Golf are quite clear on this. No shirts from other sports. *No soccer shirts, baseball shirts, hockey shirts, no bowling shirts. Get a grip, man.*

Let it be a lesson to all of us. However much you love FC Barcelona; however deeply you worship the Chicago Bulls; however greatly you respect your local pub darts league—never, ever should you wear the colors of your favorite sports team on the golf course.

Nothing wrong with covering one's head. However, the hat you choose must conform strictly with the New Rules.

In summer (but summer only), you may wear a baseball cap. If you can look as cool as Rickie Fowler, then all the better. Pay attention, though. This cap must under no circumstances have a witty golf aphorism writ upon it. Avoid like the plague any message such as "Kiss my putt!" "Cleanest balls in the business," or "I'm retired so I need my daily dose of iron."

Ideally your hat should be made by a recognized golf brand. So no Red Sox hats, no trucker hats, no rapper hats, no hats advertising motor oil or fishing stores, and certainly no novelty hats with golf flags on them.

Advice for baldies: remember to remove your hat every now and then, to give your poor pate its time in the sun. Otherwise you'll end up with an all-white crown like Stewart Cink. When he doffs his hat, it looks like he's wearing a horrendous white skullcap beneath.

And remember that visors are for jewelers. You're better off dead than being seen in one of them.

In winter, you may no longer wear a baseball hat. Instead, keep your head warm with a flat cap. For fashion tips you can always look to Samuel L. Jackson and the cool Kangol cap he wears on the course.

One last rule: nothing Scottish is permitted—especially if it involves a tartan pattern or the words "Tam" and "shanter." That's totally banned. The only exception is for grooms at bachelor parties; see rule no. 55.

When it comes to footwear, golf has a lot to answer for. Some of the sport's shoe designers are still living in the Dark Ages. *What other leisure activity that involves hiking several miles across the countryside insists you wear hard leather shoes? With tassels?*

In the old days, golfers wore brogues because they were considered more casual than the hard, plain leather shoes one wore in town. Tassels and other dodgy decorations were another sign that, while hitting golf balls, you weren't supposed to be thinking about work.

Well, that was the old days. Nowadays, *the golf shoes you choose should help you win rounds.* That means they need traction, stability, support, and comfort. A bit like hiking shoes, then. Not tasseled brogues.

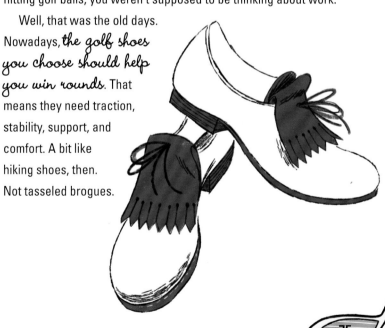

Even if the sun's beating down and burning the skin of your neck, don't be tempted to turn up your collar. It looks either loutish or preppie. *It was okay for Tom Cruise in the 1983 film Risky Business, but that's because he thought it made him look taller.* On the golf course, keep the collar down and rub in some sun cream instead.

Spanish pro Gonzalo Fernández-Castaño flips up his collar all the time. In fact, it's become a bit of a trademark for him. Listen, Gonzalo: that kind of high-collar crime may work in Madrid but you won't get away with it anywhere else.

The belt with which every self-respecting golfer should hold his trousers up is a J. Lindeberg. No other brand comes close to that super-stylish JL logo. And if you've shelled out the price of a month's club membership on said belt, at least tuck your shirt in so everyone else can admire it, too. In fact, *showing off belt buckles is the only reason a modern golfer should ever tuck in his shirt*. The best thing about this Swedish designer's belts is that you can wear them with pride both on and of the course. Either with jeans or with a suit.

Perhaps the worst belts on the PGA Tour are those of Bubba Watson. Among the über-kitsch designs he has worn is a monstrosity created by a jeweler friend of his with lettering made of pink sapphires and black diamonds that spells out Bubba's name. Apparently it set him back $25,000. Shame on you, Bubba.

Chapter Five
Other New Rules of Golf

Gambling always improves professional golf (see rule no. 60).

But if you actually want to win money, you need to adhere to certain rules:

1. Unless you have the luck of the devil, don't pick just one outright winner. Pick around five potential winners, backing some of them each way. This way, you'll still win cash even if they don't win outright. Outside of the top five players in the world rankings, you're likely to find some really attractive odds.

2. Always back players on the rise. Look for those who, over their last few tournaments, have had several top-20 placings.

3. Never underestimate the home advantage.

4. Some courses definitely suit certain players over others. So look at previous form on a course before you back a player.

5. Enjoy yourself with unusual bets. Bet on players making a hole in one, for example. Or, in spread betting, you can opt for what's known as the "disaster index." At all the majors there's always a really tricky hole where players are notorious for coming unstuck. This disaster index allows you to bet on their misfortune.

53 · GOLF MOVIES

There are some appallingly bad golf movies out there. The 2011 drama *Seven Days in Utopia* springs to mind. "If any film ever needed a Mulligan…" wrote one critic in *Time Out New York* magazine. But *if there's one golf movie that ought to be lost forever in the rough, it has to be Caddyshack 2.* This unfunny, unforgivable follow-up is a dishonor to the 1980 classic that precedes it. It's been called the worst sequel to any film… Ever made… Ever!

Golf movies aren't all bad news, however. There are at least four of them that are well worth splashing out on popcorn for.

The Legend of Bagger Vance

Will Smith plays the eponymous hero who, as mystical caddy, guides Matt Damon to sporting and personal happiness.

Tin Cup

The plot is hardly original. But this story of Kevin Costner as a washed-up former pro who has one last stab at golfing glory in order to win the heart of a rival's girlfriend pulls warmly at the heartstrings.

Happy Gilmore

Adam Sandler is genius as the ice hockey player whose slapshot earns him a place among golf's elite and helps him save his grandmother's house from the IRS.

Caddyshack

Crude, puerile, slapstick farce… This story of the eccentric characters at an exclusive country club deserves to be held up not only as the best golf film of all time, but surely one of the best comedies of all time. Without further discussion, the New Rules of Golf instantly award it an Oscar. If you've never seen it, you're not a true golfer.

Normally, the New Rules of Golf would insist that you lift your ass off the sofa and head out to the golf course pronto. But we understand that *golfers need a day off from tough exercise, too. In which case they can be forgiven for indulging in a bit of video gaming.*

However, at the time of writing, there is only one series of golf video games worth playing: *Tiger Woods PGA Tour*. It's head and shoulders above anything else available. *Don't be tempted by any of those interactive games where you pretend actually to swing the club while attached to some sort of virtual reality device.* If you want to practice your strokes but you can't get on a golf course, then you're better off putting balls across the office floor into a mug.

There's a reason why golf is so popular at bachelor and bachelorette parties. *Thanks to the handicap system, it's ideal for groups where skill levels vary enormously.* Even if you have a complete beginner and a seasoned pro in your party, you can still level the playing field so that everyone has a great time.

Here are some basic bachelor(ette) party rules:

1. Force the groom/bride-to-be to wear plus fours and a Tam o' Shanter hat

It's an ode to the game's glorious history.

2. Choose carefully the playing format for the day

Stableford is obviously ideal if you have lots of weaker players in tow. As is Scramble, where each member of a team tees off as normal before sticking with the best-lying ball, ignoring all the other shots. Players then hit their second shot from within a club's length of where the best first shot lies, and their third shot from within a club's length of where the best second shot lies, and so on until the hole is completed. To score, you add up the total number of best shots required to complete the hole.

Skins is fun, too. In this version, the winner of each hole wins cash off his fellow players. Set the prize money for each hole in advance.

If you tie on a hole, the prize money is carried over to the next hole.

What about the game known as nine points? In this, each hole (funnily enough) is worth nine points. The player who completes the hole in the fewest strokes wins five points, the runner-up wins three points, and third place gets just one point. No points for fourth place or beyond. Should two players tie for first place, they receive four points each. If all three players tie, it's three points each. There are also bonus points: shoot a birdie and you get an extra two points, while an eagle wins you an extra three points.

Otherwise, if you're all anxious to hit the 19th, you might want to consider speed golf. Here, you count both the number of strokes and the length of time it takes to complete a round. So players run between shots and carry as few clubs as possible. The overall score is calculated by adding the number of minutes to the total number of strokes.

3. Pub golf is obligatory

No bachelor/bachelorette party is complete without a celebratory round of pub golf. This classic bar-crawl game is played over either nine or 18 holes, depending on your group's drinking capacity. *Nine holes mean nine different bars must be visited, whereas 18 holes mean a very ambitious 18 different bars.*

Assign a team captain before you start. It's his or her job to choose the type of drink at each hole. In each bar (or hole), all players must attempt to down their drinks in as few gulps as possible. Scoring is the same as in real golf: fewer gulps mean a higher score. The winner is the player with the fewest number of gulps by the end of the round.

56 VIDEO ANALYSIS MUST BE USED

Nowadays most coaches arm themselves with video cameras so they can analyze their clients' strokes. And there's a good reason why: video analysis unquestionably works. It really does help you improve your game. *So don't be shy, don't be proud. Get your coach to film you and then man up as he tears your entire game to shreds.* You may cringe when you see the playback of yourself in action. But it will accelerate enormously your journey from hacker to intermediate.

57 GOLF TRIP RULES

There are three essential rules you must adhere to for booking a golf trip:

1. Are there at least 36 holes to play? If you're on vacation for a week, however well designed the course is, just 18 holes will soon get dull.

2. Does the resort have a spa that will keep your non-playing other half happy all week?

3. Does the resort have a good driving range?

You're not a real golfer until you've hit the ball-collector cart at the range. It's just too tempting. And who could ever prove that you were actually aiming for the guy inside? Besides, his cart's designed to withstand a lot of impact. So it would be churlish not to give him a lot of impact.

59 NEVER JOIN A CLUB WITHOUT A SPIKE BAR

The transition from 18th to 19th hole should be as seamless as possible. Let's be honest, on completing your round, *the first thing you need is refreshment* (and, of course, the chance to regale members with tales of your sporting brilliance while they're still fresh in your mind). That's why it's crucial to join a club with a spike bar.

Hole your putt on the 18th and, seconds later, without even changing your shoes, you'll be sipping a cold beer. How civilized is that?

60 RULES FOR WATCHING GOLF ON TELEVISION

When you have all your buddies round, watching a Major or the Ryder Cup, a sweepstake is obligatory. *Even with the dullest players in the dullest of matches, gambling will liven up proceedings enough to keep you all enthralled.*

And don't miss anything that Nick Faldo happens to be commentating on. He may have been a rubbish Ryder Cup captain, but he's arguably the best pundit on television. Fortunately his pearls of wisdom are broadcast on both sides of the Atlantic.

NEVER TEAM UP WITH YOUR OTHER HALF

61

Thanks to an alarming lack of consistency, team play among amateurs is fraught with problems at the best of times. Throw in a husband-and-wife combo and you're asking for trouble. *Down that particular fairway lie domestic strife, disaster, doom, and possibly divorce*. For that reason the New Rules of Golf insist that you never play with your other half.
Try tennis instead.

DON'T DISS THE LPGA

62

Female golf is at its highest standard ever. Yes, you can joke all you like about how men watch women's golf for the hots rather than the shots. And it's true that there are some amazingly beautiful pros gracing the courses. But, *if you can take your eyes off the legs for one second, you might just appreciate the skill of play, too.*

Hard to believe but *even in the 21st century there still exist golf clubs that prohibit female members.* At the time of writing, there were a handful of culprits, including three historical venues in the UK (The Royal St George's, Royal Troon, and Muirfield) and several in the United States.

Burning Tree Country Club, in Maryland, is perhaps the most infamous of America's same-sex clubs. Since it was founded in the 1920s, its testosterone-heavy membership roster has included presidents, congressmen, judges, military leaders, and business magnates. It not only bans female members—it doesn't even allow them on the grounds as guests. Except, that is, for a spring cocktail party and in December, when wives of members are permitted, by appointment only, in the club pro shop to pick out Christmas gifts for their husbands. (You couldn't make this up!)

Should you arrive by taxi, chauffeured by a driver with a womb (God forbid!), you would be required to step out of the taxi at the club gates and proceed on foot. Legend has it that only one female has ever gained entry uninvited to the grounds. That was back in the 1950s when the light aircraft she was flying crash-landed near the 18th hole. Burning Tree employees rapidly erected a cordon around her and the crash site—presumably to protect sensitive members from unanticipated levels of estrogen—until the police arrived and hustled her away.

In the mid-1980s, a female agent from the US Secret Service arrived at Burning Tree to carry out a security sweep for the visiting Australian prime minister who wished to play there. Barred entry, she had to stand idly in the parking lot while her male agents continued their work, communicating with her all the while by radio.

However, pressure is rising higher than ever for men-only clubs to abandon their archaic policies. In 2014, The Royal and Ancient Golf Club of St Andrews, home to the sport's governing body outside of the USA and Mexico, finally voted to accept female members. And the Augusta National Golf Club, home to the Masters, went unisex in 2012. Mind you, it didn't admit black members until 1990, so you could hardly call it a shining beacon of equality.

Influential names within the sport are rallying for equality. Just after the R&A voted to allow female members to join, Rory McIlroy (then the world No.1) said: "It's a pity that some clubs have been slow on the uptake. It doesn't matter if you are a man or a woman, black or white— everyone should have equal opportunities to do anything they want."

Another British golfer, Justin Rose, suggested that single-sex clubs ought to be excluded from hosting the Open. "If you're going to host such high-profile events, you need to conform a little bit more with what's acceptable in mainstream society," he said.

The New Rules of Golf are with McIlroy and Rose on this one. In the name of sexual equality, you should *never, ever join a club that bans women*. Besides, if you do, you won't be able to score at the 19th.

Is bigger really better? *Why do modern designers insist on creating gargantuan golf courses stretching endlessly off into the horizon?* One of the longest is the Jade Dragon Snow Mountain Golf Club in China's Yunnan province. Measuring 8,548 yards in total, this par-72 course is located at over 9,800 feet in the Himalayas. So the extra-long walks are made worse by the extra-thin air.

Eight and a half thousand yards may be feasible if you're a big-hitting pro, but *for us mere amateurs such challenges are ridiculous*. They take too long, they make you feel inadequate, and, on a summer's day, by the time you reach the 18th, you're fried to a crisp. *If you want to spend a day in the countryside, put on some big boots and go hiking instead.*

Down Under golf

The longest golf course on the planet is the Nullaboor Links, a mind-numbingly endless course stretching 848 miles along Australia's desolate Eyre Highway. It's just 18 holes, and par-72, but, even with the wind at your back, it takes a good week to complete. That's because of the huge distances you'll need to travel between each hole—sometimes well over 60 miles. The course, which stretches between Kalgoorlie in Western Australia to Ceduna in South Australia, can be played in either direction. You'll need more horsepower than a golf cart, though.

"Each hole includes a green and tee, and somewhat rugged outback-style natural terrain fairway," the owners explain. "The course provides a quintessential Australian experience."

You can say that again. Players are warned to look out for snakes, dingoes, and kangaroos. One hole claims to have Australia's largest population of southern hairy-nosed wombats. On another, there's a local crow who likes nothing better than stealing golf balls. "Try spraying smelly stuff on the balls," is the advice.

DON'T DRAW EMOTICONS ON THE BALL

There's nothing wrong with writing your initials on your golf balls. After all, when you've shelled out on expensive Titleist and they end up in the rough, you won't want your buddies trying to claim them as their own. However, *there is one thing you must never daub upon your balls—and that's smiley faces*. The New Rules of Golf are quite strict on this. Any form of emoticon is banned. Besides, smiley faces risk putting you off as you're lining up your putts.

Instead of emoticons, what you really need on your ball is a straight line, in thick, black marker pen, about an inch long. Whenever you have a tricky putt to play, adjust your ball so that the black line points directly at the cup. It makes a bigger difference than you'd think.

On the subject of golf-ball graffiti, it's worth noting that Rickie Fowler used to scrawl religious verses on his balls. This is also banned. You could write the Lord's Prayer on your Callaways or Hebrew blessings on your Srixons, and it wouldn't make any difference. *God's got better things to do than help cure your slice.*

SUPPORT YOUR LOCAL GOLF PRO SHOP

The Internet has killed so many golf-club pro shops. With cheap equipment and clothing available online, many of them simply can't compete and are going out of business. Yes, of course we all want to save money, but *we will always need the pro shop for emergency items. So it's crucial we support it.* The New Rules of Golf insist on it.

The club pro can also offer invaluable advice on your game. He's not a charity, though. There's something morally wrong about taking up his valuable time, pumping him for information on the latest drivers, then walking out and buying said drivers on the Internet. *If you're going to glean advice from him, at least give him some business in return.* And if that means you buy just your smaller items from him—balls, tees, clothing, drinks—well, it's better than nothing.

You're not a professional athlete. You're not running a marathon. Yes, *warming up for golf is important, especially the muscles you use to swing. But you don't need to make a big show of it.* Not like Spanish pro Miguel Ángel Jiménez. With a fat cigar protruding from his mouth, his pre-game routine makes him look like a bizarre mix of constipated dog, deranged flamenco dancer, and conquistador preparing for battle. It's legendary. *It's not for you, though.*

On certain golf courses, it's not just angry greenkeepers you need to look out for. Wild animals can be decidedly unfriendly, too. Golfers in warmer climates must be wary of the likes of crocodiles, alligators, and poisonous snakes. The New Rules of Golf are very straightforward on this: don't take any chances. *At the first sniff of animal danger, get the hell out of Dodge.*

Just look at what happened to poor Dougie Thomson, a British tourist who was playing golf in Mexico in 2013. He was lucky to get away with his life after being mauled by a 12-foot crocodile at a Cancun resort. He was happily playing an easy bunker shot onto the green, unaware that mortal danger was lurking in the bushes.

"My ball was in the bunker, around 10 to 15 feet from thick shrubbery," he later said from his hospital bed. "I didn't even know there was water behind the bushes. I took a shot and it landed on the green. Then I heard this noise behind me, and this huge crocodile snapped me by the thigh. I couldn't feel pain. I was in total shock. Big black eyes looking at me."

Fortunately, Thomson's buddies reacted quickly. One ran over the croc with the golf cart while the other two attacked the vicious reptile with their clubs. Eventually it retreated into the swamp, but not before taking a chunk out of Thomson's thigh. "It tore away all the muscle," he said. "My leg is like a butcher's window."

Thomson might count himself lucky compared to James Wiencek, who was playing at a South Carolina course back in 2009. The 77-year-old was retrieving a ball from a lake when a 400-pound alligator suddenly burst from below the surface, dragged him into the water, and bit off his arm below the elbow. Bleeding profusely, he was rushed to hospital while experts from wildlife control captured the beast, cut it open, and retrieved the severed arm. Unfortunately, it couldn't be reattached.

When it comes to wildlife hazards on the golf course, snakes can also cause trouble, too. In 2014, Stephen Wiese, a former US Marine, was playing a course in Lincoln, California, when he shanked his ball into tall grass. He searched for a few minutes before giving up and walking back to his golf cart. Suddenly a rattlesnake appeared out of nowhere: "No sounds, no warnings, it was just 'Bam!' I'd been hit!"

Wiese was treated in hospital and, fortunately, there were no serious repercussions. However, he's much more cautious now about hitting his balls into the rough. "I suppose it would give me a little more incentive to learn to hit the ball on the fairway," he told reporters.

Even pros golfers have brushes with wildlife. Back in 1992, Northern Irish player David Feherty was playing a practice round at the British PGA Championship when he was bitten on the finger by a poisonous adder.

"I tried to identify him," he admitted afterwards. "I tried to flick him away. He wrapped around the shaft and caught me right on the end of my finger." Feherty bravely soldiered on and completed his round but, with his finger badly swollen, he eventually had to go to the hospital.

"I considered beating the living daylights out of it," he later said. "But it probably has a wife and snakelets."

INDEX

ACKNOWLEDGMENTS

Many thanks to consultant editor Ben Cove. Ben is a journalist and former editor-at-large at *GolfPunk* magazine, a UK publication tasked with challenging the sport's elitist and archaic agenda. As a teenager, Ben was initially discouraged from playing our great game when a moody member at his local club berated him for not wearing "a proper collar" on the practice range. Undeterred, the 12-handicapper has now gone on to take alarmingly deep divots out of some of the world's best golf courses, and is a passionate exponent of golf's post-millennial wave of cool.